The Great Reset Uncovered 2021

Food crisis, Economic Collapse & Energy Shortage;
NWO – Build Back Better & The Green Deal

Rebel Press Media

1

Introduction

Europe will end up in a total system crisis - Right now Germany is already blaming 'cyber attacks' (by 'the Russians', of course), which for the time being will have to prepare the population for a major war - '0.025% deaths does not justify destruction of the world economy'

The 'Great Reset' of our stable and prosperous society, deliberately set in motion under the guise of an airway virus, is about to be felt even harder. More and more indications suggest that Europe is heading for a food crisis with sky-high prices. Meanwhile, politicians and the press continue to pass on, justify and sometimes even applaud all the responsibility for the misery that has already been caused and which is on the way.

The UN Food and Agriculture Organization's (FAO) Food Price Index (FFPI) rose 2.3 points (2.2%) in one month to 107.5 in December 2020, the seventh consecutive increase. The FFPI stood at just 53.1 points in 2002, peaked at 131.9 in 2011 due to the financial crisis, before falling to just below 100.

Disclaimer

Copyright 2021 by REBEL PRESS MEDIA – All Rights Reserved

This document aims to provide exact and reliable information in regard to the topic and issue covered. The publication is sold with the idea that the publisher is not required to render accounting, officially permitted, or otherwise, qualified services. If advice is necessary, legal or professional, a practiced individual in the profession should be ordered – from a Declaration of Principles which was accepted and approved equally by a Committee of the American Bar Association and a Committee of the Publishers and Associations.

In no way is it legal to reproduce, duplicate, or transmit any part of this document in either electronic means or in printed format. Recording of this publication is strictly prohibited and any storage of this document is not allowed unless with written permission from the publisher. All rights reserved.

The presentation of the information is without contract or any type of guarantee assurance. The trademarks that are used are without any consent, and the publication of the trademark is without permission or backing by the trademark owner. All trademarks and brands within this book are for clarifying purposes only and are owned by the owners themselves, not affiliated with this document. We don't encourage any substance abuse and we cannot be held responsible for any partaking in illegal activities.

Our other books

Check out our other books for other unreported news, exposed facts and debunked truths, and more.

Join the exclusive Rebel Press Media Circle!

You will get a new updates about the unreported reality delivered in your inbox every Friday.

Sign up here today:

https://campsite.bio/rebelpressmedia

Table of Contents

Chapter 1: The upcoming food, energy and banking crisis

As politicians seize on perfectly normal, natural and for the vast majority of people harmless corona mutations to extend and/or expand lockdown measures and restrictions on freedom, the food supply lines will face similar problems to what the electronic industry is now facing (major shortage of microchips).

In Germany, there are already warnings that fruit and vegetable shortages are imminent. They have also already identified a so-called cause: cyber-attacks, which of course "the Russians" will be blamed for. The wretched World Economic Forum of Klaus Schwab, the evil genius behind the 'Great Reset', also expects cyber-attacks on the electricity grid and the banking sector.

Blame others for what you cause yourself

Also, slowly but surely becoming unaffordable basic food and energy, coupled with major problems with bank accounts and online payments, should get you ready to agree to a major war, probably against Russia. In reality, the energy disruptions will be caused by the switch away from coal, oil and gas, because per se switching to unreliable and expensive wind, solar and biomass is required. In addition, the next mega banking crisis has been in the making for years, which will be used to push through a complete digital payment system with a digital euro.

It is the old, familiar historical concept that has been applied so often: blame the party you consider the enemy for the problems you have caused yourself, and you are assured of their support. Unfortunately, hardly anyone reads the history books anymore, or they refuse to learn from them ('this time we'll do it better', 'this time things will be different') because they think they are so much smarter. (Our take on this? Just the opposite).
Or you have studied for it, and apply the socially manipulating and subversive neo-Marxist tactics that authoritarian and dictatorial regimes have used so often before in an extremely refined way to your own people, and let them be grateful for it too.

Was there any inside information, or is this a devious plan?

In this regard, the American economist Martin Armstrong once again points to the 'Event 201' pandemic simulation in October 2019, well known to many by now, where everything done from 2020 onwards was discussed, drafted and worked out in detail in advance, complete with the deliberate sowing of fear and panic over a mere coronavirus.
'Did they have foreknowledge of the future, or is there a devious plan to reduce population and CO2, conveniently causing mass genocide, as some now believe? Such conspiracy theories always arise when you have secret meetings and elite groups who feel

themselves exalted above the lower people, whom they consider the 'Great Scum'.

However, conspiracy theories are long gone, since all these evil plans can be read, heard and seen openly in the publications of these organizations like the WEF. Although some of them, such as "In 2030 you will own nothing and you will be happy" have been taken offline again after they caused quite a stir. That will not stop these authoritarian bureaucrats from imposing this dystopian future on you and me (but not on themselves) in 2030 (but probably much earlier).

Chapter 2: Major social unrest due to food crisis (and possibly war)

In any case, it is certain that between now and 2024, food shortages and skyrocketing prices are coming anyway. 'This will lead to major social and political unrest,' writes Armstrong.

'The mismanagement by the EU government could well be their undoing. After all, during the course of this crisis, because of that mismanagement, many people have lost their jobs because they have had to stay at home, and simultaneously their purchasing power has fallen. This is the worst possible outcome, and that's why we can wonder if these leaders are really that stupid, or just that devious?'

Devious, because this systemic crisis has been planned to all intents and purposes, including fully controlling and directing the mainstream media, with the intention of creating a dictatorial EU superstate that will be (and in many ways already is) a technocratic mix of the former Soviet system and today's communist China.

Stupid, because they think that this 'Great Reset / Build Back Better / Green New Deal' coup against free society will also succeed in the longer term, so that by 2030 the Mark and Sigrids of our time will have realized their dreamed climate paradise.

Evidently these people have no sense of reality anymore, because otherwise they would at least have to consider that with this all-and-everything disruptive course nothing can remain of our civilization in 2030 at the latest.

In any case, the world is not prepared for a food crisis, Armstrong believes, which will no doubt be caused by the maintenance of corona measures. The shortages will be particularly acute in the larger cities. The high VAT and taxes in Europe will be the final blow for many. Then supermarkets need not be stocked for only a few days for large-scale panic, chaos and violence to break out.

According to the economist, stock market speculators will be blamed, but we could think that (also) a political culprit will be identified, probably Russian President Vladimir Putin. If so, it is convenient if you have already provoked a major regional war in, say, Ukraine, and possibly in the Middle East, before then. After all, we have seen how easy supply chains are to disrupt by just one container ship (Suez Canal).

Bill Gates is one of the biggest contributors to this crisis Armstrong then cites another "conspiracy theory" that Bill Gates is now the largest owner of farmland in the US. True or not, it is in any case proven that he has actually 'bought' the WHO and has it in his pocket, as well as the American CDC, and presumably all similar institutes in Europe. In addition, he has financial interests in every major pharmaceutical company, and is the driving force behind the GAVI vaccine alliance. So Gates will undeniably be one of the biggest contributors to the years-long crisis, but the Western media, co-controlled by him, will never be allowed to write that. In the past decade, hundreds of thousands of farms have disappeared in both America and Europe, largely because their existence was made impossible by ever-increasing taxes and ever-stricter 'climate' rules and laws. In this way, governments were able to get hold of large amounts of land at ridiculously low prices for, among other things, housing, 'sustainable' energy and 'nature restoration' projects. This long-standing anti-farming policy threatens to exponentially intensify the coming food crisis.

0.025% deaths does not justify destruction of world economy

'Meanwhile, there is a rush to vaccinate everyone against a disease that is no more deadly than the flu,' Armstrong continued. 'The number of Covid deaths is so exaggerated that our politicians are either the dumbest people in the world or the most devious. During the Spanish flu, there were 50 million deaths, 3.125% of the world's population then (1.6 billion). Now there are 7.8 billion people, and even 2 million dead are only 0.02564% of that. This in no way justifies the destruction of the world economy.'

Nuremberg agreements ignored and even reversed
'The mainstream press simply applauds the lockdowns and terrorizes the public. It is coming to light that the vaccinations protect no one from contracting Covid, and may even put them in greater danger once the population is crushed by one of the new mutations. Meanwhile, the pharmaceutical companies are immune from all liability. In Nuremberg, all world leaders agreed to ban such medical experiments on the population if they had not yet (or not sufficiently) been tested on animals. The vaccines that are now being injected have not even been tested on rats or mice.'
(This is partly due to far-left, Marxist 'woke' thinking, which has stripped humans of all higher spirituality, and sees them as nothing more than some sort of biological machine that in no way transcends animal life. Indeed, by using humans as guinea pigs and not animals, humans are placed below animals. It goes without saying that this reprehensible anti-human thinking prepares the way for a massacre, a genocide, such as the world has never known before and will probably never know again, because there will simply be too few of us left).

Lord Sumption, a former judge of the British Supreme Court, was already very critical of the totalitarian corona measures several times last year. Now he warns that these measures could take as long as 10 years, because governments can no longer reverse their decisions without extreme loss of face. Our expectation is that if the current policies are indeed continued for another 10 years and even tightened, by 2030 at the latest nothing at all will be left of our once free and prosperous society.

Sumption cites a historical precedent. After WW-2, food rations continued in Great Britain for 9 years. 'People wanted that, because they were behind social control. But in 1951 the Labour party completely lost the majority, because people who had 5 years or long social control behind them were fed up. Sooner or later that's going to happen in this country now.'

The former chief justice was responding to statements by government officials that all measures, including lockdowns, social distancing and mouthguards, will remain in place unabated until everyone is vaccinated. The British government decided recently to extend all measures at least until October. Health Minister Matt Hancock declined to say whether there would be another extension after that.

It is so serious that even politicians no longer dare to offer a well-founded protest.

'You have not failed in this battle, since it is your sacred duty to make your own contribution by taking the side of Good. Others, addicted to corruptions, or blinded by an infernal hatred of our Lord, have chosen the side of Evil.'

'Do not think that the children of darkness operate in an honest manner, nor be shocked that they make use of deception. Or do you sometimes believe that Satan's followers are honest, sincere and loyal? The Lord has warned us about the devil, who "was a murderer of men from the beginning, and stands not in truth, for there is no truth in him. When he speaks the lie, he speaks according to his nature, for he is a liar and the father of lies.' (John 8:44)

Lord Sumption points out that politicians and scientists who oppose the lockdown policy "are subjected to an extremely unpleasant personal smear campaign. I know of many who would rather not put their heads above the parapet. From the very beginning when I spoke out I began to get emails from politicians who agreed with me but dared not say anything themselves. I think this is a very serious situation.'

It is now clear to many people that a typical respiratory virus, which is dangerous only to a small group of elderly and vulnerable people (and which has an established survival rate of 99.7%) is being exploited to push through a particular agenda, the 'Great Reset' under the communist UN Agenda-2030. Anyone who openly disagrees is targeted with draconian methods. People should be allowed to express their differences,' says the judge. 'If you can enforce social distancing only by beating people on their heads with sticks, then it's not worth it.'

Chapter 4: End phase of our civilization?

Nevertheless, polls (as far as they can still be trusted) show that most people agree that their society is being changed and deformed forever. That is the signal for politicians to push through even tougher and stricter measures in the coming years, under the guise of new viruses and/or 'the climate', which will put an end to the last remnants of freedom forever, and soon also to our current prosperity.

Welcome to the beginning of the harshest and most anti-human dictatorship this world has ever known. And you yourself voted for it. Hence our repeated question whether our society has sometimes become suicidal. Every civilization comes to an end – usually quite suddenly – very often because people let totalitarian leaders do their thing and often even cooperate with them. It is painful to observe, but perhaps now it is our turn to go down.

 24 world leaders call for swift establishment of global WHO vaccine dictatorship

No one is safe until everyone is safe' actually means that every world citizen will soon be required to be vaccinated - Top New Agers expected the beginning of the new Luciferian world order in 2012: 2012 is actually 2021?
24 world leaders, including German Chancellor Angela Merkel, French President Macron and British Prime

Minister Johnson, have signed a letter calling for a treaty that would allow for a global WHO vaccine dictatorship. Of course, this is not stated literally, but it overwhelmingly boils down to the fact that all countries, under the guise of "pandemic preparedness," must surrender their national and medical sovereignty to a global government. This is exactly what we warned about in January 2020, namely that the coronavirus will be misused to establish a dictatorial communist world government, which we firmly believe will become the harshest and most anti-human regime this planet has ever known, although it will present itself as exactly the opposite.

The most shocking evidence of this is the openly expressed statement "No one is safe until everyone is safe", in itself an absurd premise, since life does not work that way, never has and never WILL work that way, since everyone would have to be permanently forced to stay home. Then we ignore for a moment that most accidents happen precisely at home.

At a time when Covid-19 has exploited our weaknesses and divisions, we must seize this opportunity and come together as a global community for peaceful cooperation that extends beyond this crisis, is one of the media's now chewed-out arguments for ending 'isolationism and nationalism.

The ultimate goal: mandatory vaccination for all world citizens
The rest of the media surrounding covid-19 and the great reset, too, is nothing but the by now tiresome and hollow blather about forcing unity, supposedly because this would be best for humanity, when in reality something completely different is being realized and a horrible dystopia will be created with it.

Indeed, 'No one is safe until everyone is safe' is a thinly veiled threat to people who do not want to be injected with experimental gene-manipulating substances marketed as 'vaccines' to men (and women and children). It indicates that world leaders have long since decided where they want to go, namely, mandatory vaccination, on pain of total exclusion from society (and, in time, also on pain of having all your rights and all your possessions taken away, presumably followed by forced incarceration in a 're-education camp').

If the first pandemic doesn't convince you, then the second pandemic will.

This compulsion to vaccinate is going to happen, you can be sure of that, no matter how often it is still denied. After all, Bill Gates was already openly gloating about it during a TV interview: 'If the first pandemic didn't convince you, the second will.
So he already knew last year that at least two pandemics are planned, the second of which will be the final blow to the population's mental health, which is

already under great pressure. The latter will then shout and scream for 'safety' and demand from their governments that the vaccine refusers - who will be falsely blamed for this second pandemic and the subsequent lockdowns - are all removed from society at all costs.

That second pandemic could also be the by Gates' announced "bio terrorist attack," most likely just another false flag / propaganda operation that critical observers believe may be caused precisely by vaccinations. Indeed, scientists and other experts have repeatedly warned that the vaccines can disable a crucial part of the human immune system, leaving vaccinated people defenseless when the corona and other respiratory viruses return in the fall or winter. Some therefore feel that the vaccines themselves are these "bio terror" weapons that Gates warned about in 2020.

Chapter 5: The last world empire

Institutional Christianity

The announced WHO/WEF/UN/EU dictatorship will be a central part, is nothing less than the establishment of the "Realm of Antichrist" (better, Realm of "the Beast," because the term "antichrist" does not appear anywhere in the entire apocalyptic book of Revelation, and therefore does not refer to a single person) foretold in the Bible. Although I have little respect for his denomination, I agree with him in this regard.

The sad thing is that it is precisely institutionalized Christianity that enables, facilitates and promotes the coming of that final, transnational, anti-Christian world empire (and this too, by the way, is foretold in biblical prophecies). Pope Francis already called for a "universal vaccine for all humanity" last year, even suggesting that not getting yourself vaccinated is a (mortal) sin. Most other Christian movements, from Protestant conservative to evangelical and Pentecostal, more or less agree with him. Consider also the many Christian parties, ministers and government leaders who are right behind this agenda and are carrying it out.

All over the world millions of Christians have been looking forward to "the end times. Now that the time indeed seems to have come, most of them suddenly seem to want to know nothing about it, only because the coming of the foretold kingdom of the Beast will take place in a different way and partly with different methods than they have been led to believe by 'ear tickling treaties' all this time. What's more: many are actually working on it out of full conviction.

New Agers have been expecting the Luciferian world order for nearly a century

On March 28, 2009, so almost to the day 12 years ago, we wrote that high-ranking New Agers predicted that in 2012 under President Barack Obama the "Luciferian world order" would be established. Did they not mean 2012, but perhaps 2021?

'Mankind is moving toward a new civilization and a New Age world culture, which will become known as the Age of Light,' wrote New Ager Tom Carney in 2009 in 'Thoughtline,' pointing to the infamous occultist Alice Bailey (whose NGO Lucis Trust is recognized by the UN) and her 'New Group of World Servants' (note also the pyramid and the rainbow), founded as early as 1924, and her 'Great Plan' for humanity. In the view of theosophists like Bailey and many other New Agers like Helena Blavatsky, the one who will bring this 'Light' is the 'Light Bringer', Lucifer, referred to in the Bible as the devil, Satan.

There are theories that state that the mRNA vaccines are necessary to modify our DNA in such a way that we will all soon be fully controllable, manipulable and automatically obeying followers of this false light.

21

Whether this is really so remains to be seen, but the New Age magazine 'Innerchange' literally spoke in its first issue of 2009 of a 'Lucifer archetype' as 'the new human being' who would populate the earth in the very near future.

It is speculation, but possibly the 12 years after that were used to first place these 'archetypes' in powerful positions in national governments, supranational organizations, and religious institutions so that at the right time, perhaps taking advantage of the deliberately instilled fear of an average respiratory virus, they could seize total power to realize this Luciferian world order, this biblical 'realm of the Beast'.

Although millions of people in the West have woken up to the great danger of the UN/EU/IMF/WEF/NATO globalists, we are still in the minority.

Certainly in europe, most people still blindly believe the propaganda of mainstream political parties and media, even though numerous of their blatant lies have been exposed, especially in recent years. For those whose eyes have been opened, the persistent inanity and sometimes shocking stupidity of gullible fellow humans can sometimes be quite frustrating.

Indeed, with a little background research and critical thinking, it can be concluded that the late Wuhan coronavirus pandemic is likely a deliberately created crisis designed to subject all nations to a totalitarian world government.

The globalists' agenda can be summed up with one term: 'Order from Chaos'. Analyst Brandon Smith is by no means the first to point out that 'every crisis is created or exploited to manipulate the public into consent. But assent to what?'

Chapter 6: The banking crisis

Upcoming financial mega-crisis will be used for final push through communist 'Great Reset'

While the focus of both government and media is still almost entirely on corona, extremely worrying developments are taking place in the EU in the background, which are likely to have very far-reaching consequences for our prosperity and purchasing power already in the short to medium term.

The ECB is going to buy more government debt in the coming months, because interest rates on government bonds have started to rise again.

Also, the de facto technically already bankrupt banking system is in even bigger trouble because of the manufactured corona crisis.

'The only thing holding the European Commission together anymore is the magic money tree called the ECB,' writes analyst Alasdair Macleod.

If you have ever taken two classes in economics, you should know where such a "money tree" always inevitably leads: "This is a horror show in the making.

The EUSSR is a fait accompli in political and financial terms

Critics often mockingly describe the European Union as the EUSSR, and this is certainly not an exaggeration in the year 2021 - on the contrary.

Politically, the EU has long been functioning exactly like the former Soviet Union: the Politburo, an unelected club of bureaucrats called the European Commission, determines the policy, and gives its 'wishes' (=orders) to the European Council of Heads of Government, who debate them for form's sake, and then take these orders to their own - in name only - independent countries, where the parliaments, reduced to 'yes-men', always automatically put a stamp of approval on them.

To keep up the pretence of a European democracy, the EU itself also has a 'parliament', of which all the members receive sky-high salaries, bonuses and pensions for taking part in this great play, and remaining silent about the fact that in reality they have nothing, absolutely nothing to say.

The only time this parliament ever seemed to have any 'power' was when it sent a European Commission home, but that was - especially in retrospect - most likely just staged, because it was at that time that the European public started to wake up to the 'socialist' (in the Marxist sense) nature and design of the EU.

Recently, the ECB quietly took the next step toward the inevitable destruction of the euro, the euro/Target-2 system, and itself. The bank decided to buy more government bonds in the coming months, contrary to earlier announcements, because interest rates are rising again worldwide. If this trend continues it will cause the bankruptcy of the entire eurozone network. 'And that network is like a mouthful of rotten apples,' says Macleod. 'It is the result of not only a failing system, but also of policies to save Spain from rising interest rates in 2012.'

Whatever it takes', the euro currency will be 'saved' at the citizens' expense

At that time, then ECB President Mario Draghi spoke his infamous words that he would save the euro "whatever it takes. What he didn't tell us was that the price of this "whatever it takes" would have to be cough up by European savers and pension funds in the first place.

Because of the ever-increasing debt, Christine Lagarde's intervention must necessarily be even greater than that of her predecessor Draghi. Ultimately, all Europeans will have to pay heavily for this through a substantial and permanent loss of their purchasing power and prosperity. The tinsel years of prosperity of the EU member states are almost over.

Lagarde puts Draghi's 'whatever it takes' into even higher gear. The ECB, which claims to be 'independent' but is a political institution through and through, has really only ever served one purpose, and that is to ensure that the uncontrolled spending of the southern member states in particular is always covered.

An ingenious system was devised for this purpose: Target-2

Italy and Spain alone owe this ECB system almost €1 trillion. Germany, Luxembourg, Finland and the Netherlands, on the other hand, are owed about € 1.6 trillion by this system, the lion's share of which (over € 1 trillion) is owed by Germany. *(In fact, tiny Luxembourg can be seen as a bank disguised as an independent state, one of the many tricks the ECB uses to make the EU's financial situation look rosier.)*

Large megabanks technically already bankrupt
By buying up government bonds, the ECB itself already has a debt of € 345 billion, partly due to the covert financing of the rapidly increasing French government deficit. France can now be counted among the PIIGS countries, but this will never be officially admitted because France is considered a "systemically important" state.

Meanwhile, France's burdens are beginning to weigh more and more heavily on the euro system, not least because the French mega-bank Société Générale is technically effectively bankrupt, as are Deutsche Bank and Italy's Unicredit, for that matter.

What the statistics don't show is that the Bundesbank has already bought up many billions in German government debt on behalf of the ECB. The ever-growing imbalance in the Target-2 system has come about because Italy, Spain, Greece and Portugal in particular have been saddled with more and more 'bad' debts, or debts that can and will never be repaid.

The result was that the 'zombie' banking systems in these countries had to be put on a permanent ECB drip.

Bunch of drunks in the gutter
The bad debts and other 'bad assets' were passed on to the euro system (and therefore in particular to Germany, Finland, the Netherlands and Luxembourg) at the time of the 'bailout' of Greece, and then the bailout of the Italian banks, which was hidden from the public.

What is not in the statistics is an even many times higher amount of €8.31 trillion (total probably more than €10 trillion) in short-term funding, which in the eurozone needs virtually no cover.

In short, it means that you, for example, with an average annual income of € 36,000, can get a loan from the bank of € 1 million without blinking an eye, and the bank manager then says to you: "See what you can pay back, and when..." What do you think, will this bank stay healthy for long? And will a central bank that then

keeps these banks afloat for years also stay healthy for
a long time?

'Like a bunch of drunks trying to hoist themselves
staggeringly out of the gutter, the stock prices of
eurozone banks have risen along with the markets. But
their ratings remain so appallingly poor,' observes
Macleod. The situation is now so dire that if one big
eurozone bank were to fail, the whole system would
collapse like a house of cards.

EU a 'failing state': purchasing power will be wiped out

'The EU has all the signs of a failing state,' the analyst
continued. This was particularly evident in the EU's
reaction to the Brexit, which can really only be
described as taking revenge in a way that is as obtuse as
it is childish, regardless of the painful consequences for
the bloc itself.

Also, the EU is unlikely to emerge from lockdowns this
year, which means that all member states will have to
continue taking on unprecedented new debt to keep
their economies afloat. The consequences of extremely
damaging policies will be even more severe for Europe
than for the U.S. and China.

Large parts of the economy - especially small business
owners- are on the verge of collapse. Added to the
developments in the commodity markets (oil, metals,

food, etc.) and the gigantic increase in the money supply, all this will lead to a worldwide loss of purchasing power. The EU, thanks to its own structure, policies and actions, is completely lagging behind the economic recovery, which is already in full swing in China.

'And because the financing of everything rests on the shoulders of the ECB, the crisis in the EU will definitely start there. It will certainly bring down most of the banking system...

It won't take a very sharp rise in interest rates to wipe that out.' And then the true value of the 'value' and 'assets' that the big Eurozone banks claim to have on their balance sheets is also revealed: 'essentially NOTHING.'

No wonder capital flight from the Eurozone has accelerated. Money always flees from places with bad and wasteful policies, and where it will soon be worth nothing.

The economy is deliberately inflated to achieve communist Great Reset

If you are wondering: but why aren't they trying to prevent this? Then my answer is: because I think the system is being deliberately blown up. A digital euro is already in the works, and it should at some point replace all cash. This new digital money system will presumably be introduced during or just after the impending financial mega-crisis, and will be gradually linked to everything (ID/passport, debit card, Covid card, etc.). All debts will be forfeited, after which all 'assets', all property, all finances, of all companies and individuals, will fall to the state.

Then the 'Great Reset', the transformation of the once successful E.E.C. free trade bloc into a European Soviet Union with a technocratic and deeply communist system, will be complete.

Then our prosperity and all our freedoms and possessions will be done for good. (And you as an entrepreneur were so happy with the promised compensation of 100% of your fixed costs by the government!

Do you really not realize in which trap you all have stepped? That you in this planned economy soon nothing more to say about your own business and survival?)

To get an idea of how 'pleasant' life will be for us then, take a look at the history books, I would say. For most people, however, such an appeal will fall on deaf ears.

Recently, Europeans voted even more massively for nominally 'liberal' parties, which for years have implemented almost exclusively neo-Marxist EU policies.

Since the people want to remain blind for the inevitable consequences, there seems to be only one thing left, to our great regret, and that is to suffer a lot of pain (again) to bring the people back to their senses.

With the hope that our surviving (grand)children after this terrible systemic crisis will have learned from these rock-hard lessons and will be able and willing to build a much healthier society, a society where there is no place anymore for Big Banks, Big Pharma, Big Tech, Big Military and Big Government, in other words: for Big Corruption.

Chapter 7: The green deal

*To achieve the climate goals, a communist eco-dicature
will be established, which will end all our freedoms and
a very large part of our current prosperity.
Economist DB Research: 'Brussels tells unfair story to
citizens' - Painful measures very near: loss of freedom of
transport, heating, home, food*

An analysis by Deutsche Bank strongly criticizes the
European Union for presenting the 'Green Deal' to the
public in far too rosy a light, and for having 'an unfair
debate' about it.

DB wants Brussels to let Europeans know that
implementing the Green Deal will mean an economic
and social mega-crisis, that some kind of eco-
dictatorship will be needed to impose all the measures,
and that we will permanently lose a huge portion of our
prosperity.

This is what we have been warning about for years: the
EU's 'climate plans' will have zero effect on 'climate
change', but will turn our continent into a backward
area with widespread poverty, in which we will have no
freedom whatsoever.

The monstrously expensive 'Green Deal' poses
enormous risks to prosperity, the economy and
democracy, according to DB. Those risks should be told
honestly to the people, and not withheld, as is

happening now. At least that is what Eric Heymann, senior economist at Deutsche Bank Research, writes.

Brussels presents the Green Deal as "a new growth strategy" that will lead to "a fair and prosperous society," but that claim is highly dubious. It all sounds good on paper, but in order to achieve a truly climate-neutral Europe by 2050, the entire economy, as well as the entire political and judicial system, must be fundamentally changed.

Koire is also the author of the book "Behind the Green Mask - UN Agenda 21. Agenda 21 was signed by 178 countries and the Vatican in 1992. With this agenda, a globalist power elite wants to gain total control over all land, water, vegetation, minerals, construction, means of production, food and energy.

Law enforcement, education, information, and the people themselves must also come under this complete control.

So far, the implications of the EU climate agenda are "still relatively abstract," and for most households "still acceptable. But that is about to change. Drastic interventions are coming that will put an end to the choice of free transport, the size of houses, the way we heat, the possession of electronic consumer goods, and the consumption of meat and tropical fruits, for example. Also, employment will be hit hard.

Taxes on energy will rise much further, making heating and transport extremely expensive. Heymann warns that there are no adequate technologies available to maintain our current level of prosperity.

We know that eco-dictatorship is a nasty word, but we have to ask ourselves to what extent we are prepared to accept a kind of eco-dictatorship in order to become climate neutral.

For example, what should we do with property owners who refuse to make their homes and buildings climate neutral?'*

(*The elite found an answer to that in 2020: seize an average respiratory virus for a series of lockdowns with severe restrictions, and thus put hundreds of thousands of farmers and businesses on the state drip. They are thus effectively expropriated through the back door.

The state thus gains total power to make tough demands on the restarting of these businesses, if they survive the crisis and/or get permission to do so).
Are you willing to deny your children the prosperity you did enjoy?

A better question is: are you and I willing to deprive our (grand)children of at least the same prosperity and freedom we enjoyed until the early 2020s? Are we prepared to tell them soon that they will have to live in permanent poverty and oppression, while the

inhabitants of countries such as China and Russia, who
do not want to demolish their societies to counteract a
perfectly natural gas (CO2) that is actually much needed
for all life - and of which there are still historically low
levels in the atmosphere - will soon have a much higher
level of prosperity and well-being?
And how are you going to explain to them, in the midst
of a period of Global Cooling, freezing cold and food
shortages, that it was all 'really necessary' to counteract
so-called global warming?

The Green Deal will lead to the demise of the EU
Our expectation? Many Europeans are not going to put
up with this. The harsher and more coercive the EU
climate dictatorship will become, and the more wealth
and freedom it will take away from citizens, the greater
the resistance will be. Eventually there will be large
revolts, governments will be overthrown, and countries
will leave the EU, which will then collapse with a
thunderous roar, and end up on the garbage heap of
history.

Exactly where this unholy, anti-democratic, always
lying, cheating and thieving union belongs. Then the
next generation can start rebuilding on the gigantic
ruins the eurocrats will have left behind, and hopefully
have learned from the capital blunders the European
politicians have made.

A German farmer is sounding the alarm on behalf of numerous European colleagues about the "Green New Deal" of the European Commission and "climate czar" Frans Timmermans. Brussels wants Europe to become so-called 'climate neutral' by 2050, and for that modern agriculture has to be eliminated. If this plan goes through, it will lead to inefficient, much less 'green' agriculture, to poorer harvests, and therefore much higher food prices. This will cause widespread hunger and poverty, especially among lower-income people. In May last year, more details of the 'European Green Deal' were revealed. The European Commission wants to turn society completely upside down, and make the "transition fair and inclusive" for everyone. However, at least one group is completely excluded from this: farmers.

'Farm to Fork' is the name of the strategy chosen to reform agriculture in Europe. The goals of this strategy are completely "unrealistic," writes German farmer Marcus Holtkoetter for the Global Farmer Network. 'Farmers would have to reduce their crop protection products by half in the next decade, and fertilizer by 20%. As much as a quarter of all existing farmland should be used for 'organic' production.'
'But of course none of this would disrupt people's meals,' the farmer continued cynically.
Food will become more expensive

Europeans are blessed with an abundance of food (although the quality can be questioned, especially for

refined foods), especially since agriculture can be counted among the most modern and efficient in the world. The soil is fertile, the harvests almost always of high quality. 'Due to intensive agriculture, we have achieved excellent results. As a result, we do not have problems of hunger and malnutrition, which plague people with less luck in other societies.'
'What the European Commission is now proposing amounts to smaller harvests. For consumers, this will lead directly to one thing: higher prices. Food will become more expensive.'

Ever smaller harvests

Another big problem is that farmers, who are already struggling, will earn even less because of lower harvests and thus lower sales. 'The commission does not understand that its poor approach to agriculture will lead to farmers who can no longer make ends meet quitting. Once this happens, the lower harvests will become even smaller.'

This is the opposite of what the commission says it wants to achieve, which is "a sustainable" economy and agriculture. Even more important is the question of where our food should come from then, if European farmers are no longer allowed to produce enough of it. The European Green Deal will therefore inevitably lead to even more inefficient agriculture in countries with less fertile and productive land.

What is "green" about growing fewer crops on more land?

That might fill the bellies in a Europe with fewer farmers, and possibly even ease the conscience of the activists and bureaucrats in Brussels. But it will absolutely NOT help the climate. Our goal should be to grow more food on less land. The EU's approach, guided not by science but by ideology, will actually lead to growing less food on more land. What is 'green' about that?

Bear in mind that by 2050 the world's population will have increased by a further 2 billion people. They will also need to eat. It would be quite a task to do that with the current efficient agricultural methods, but it could still be done. Agriculture has proven to be very innovative in recent decades.

EU sees citizen as a problem to be solved

But what farmers do NOT need is even more rules and even more restrictions. That would be the final blow for many, and would endanger food security in Europe. The worst thing is that the European Green Deal seems to assume that farmers are the enemies of nature conservation. It treats us as a problem to be solved, rather than an ally in a common cause.'

'We work hard to be as 'green' as possible. On my farm, we produce some of our electricity with solar panels. We use GPS and other technologies to reduce our waste in fertilization and weed control. We plant crops to protect the soil from erosion. We plant flower beds to attract insects that pollinate crops, and improve biodiversity.'

'The best way to prevent positive innovation is to make sure farmers can't make ends meet. So for farmers, and for everyone else, the European Green Deal is a very bad deal.'

Insects should replace meat consumption in light of the disastrous, wealth-destroying 'Green New Deal'

One part of the EU's welfare- and freedom-destroying "Green New Deal," hobbyhorse of Marxist Eurocommissioner Frans Timmermans, has now gone into effect. The European Food Safety Authority has approved the sale and consumption of insects such as grasshoppers, crickets and mealworms for human consumption. The climate dictatorship in Brussels, by wiping out livestock farming, wants to sharply reduce the consumption of meat in the coming years, and force the population to switch to alternative food coupons.

'There is a good chance that we will get the green light in the next few weeks,' the secretary general of the International Platform of Insects for Food and Nutrition, Christophe Derrien, responded to The Guardian. He is looking forward to the moment when insects are both for single sale in stores and also incorporated into other products such as snacks, pasta and burgers. His argument: insects are a good source of protein, but their production "does not harm the planet.

The promotion of consuming insects by all kinds of globalist organizations, cultural institutions and the media is done to prepare the Western population for a drastically lower standard of living, which will result from the disastrous 'Green New Deal'. The implementation of this monstrously expensive program, which will forever end the post-war accumulated prosperity, will intensify the deep economic recession/depression resulting from the corona measures.

This is also why the Economist, mouthpiece of the international left-liberal elite, promotes eating insects. However, the question is whether any of these 'top' figures, who have deliberately set in motion the downfall of our free society, will ever put an insect in their mouths themselves (except for the usual staged propaganda photos). For you know: in every communist dictatorship the rulers have exempted themselves from all the harsh measures with which they oppress the common people.

41

Extreme leftist green climate deal EU costs family over 5100 euros per year

A 'man on the moon moment for the EU' is called Frans Timmermans' Green climate deal. The proposals of the climate pope of the EU Politburo are so extreme and insane that the comparison with the moon is indeed correct. If only half of Timmermans' communist climate dictatorship is realized, we will all figuratively go 'to the moon'. The EU wants to spend € 575 billion every year to turn the whole society upside down and make it 'climate neutral'. And who is going to pay for that? Exactly, the citizens. Per inhabitant € 1280, - per year and per average family € 5120, - per year. And in return we get the gradual total destruction of our prosperity and freedom.

Derk Jan Eppink recently asked in Brussels who in the next 20 years should pay the € 11.5 trillion (three times the GDP of Germany) that Timmermans' climate dystopia will cost. No one answered him. Presumably, as always, it is mainly the Netherlands that is considered, because we are already the largest net contributors to the EU, and guarantee, through various emergency funds, some € 100 billion to keep the financially failed euro project afloat.

The Fourth Reich is going to rule with an iron fist

By the way, 80% of our laws already come from Brussels and Strasbourg. So that European Fourth 'Reich', or European Union of Soviet Socialist Republics, actually already exists. But from 2020 onwards, this communist Reich will really rule with a heavy fist, all under the guise of the fake "saving the climate", but mainly to save the banks again. Major Wall Street names are warning that the next financial mega-crisis, the systemic crisis we have been writing about for years, is now literally on the verge of breaking out.

What we can still do to prevent losing everything is to revolt en masse, as the peasants now want to do again on December 18. We as a people have to say 'enough is enough', and break as soon as possible with the political elite that knowingly hands over our country, our prosperity, our culture, our freedom and our democracy to an extremist regime in Brussels that is obviously hostile to us.

Don't say in 5 years' time that you weren't warned, when you will have to use all your remaining income to survive at all, and that in houses that will hardly be able to be lit and heated because of the sky-high climate taxes. Europe's Green Deal = end of prosperity, end of welfare, end of freedom, and welcome to totalitarian dictatorship. And all in the name of a climate crisis that is completely out of whack.

Greta's Greenpeace climate activists want to turn the West into modern-day Killing Fields

The ever-increasing trend in the West toward communist socialism and a climate dictatorship reminds American top economist Marin Armstrong of the infamous Khmer Rouge leader and mass murderer Pol Pot, whose ideal society consisted of poor, subsistence farmers with as little money, wealth and possessions as possible. 'He embraced Marxism and viewed modern society as evil, something we hear again now in the climate movement.'

During his attempts to subject all of Cambodia to his ideas, 1.5 million to 2 million people died of starvation. Opponents of Pot's regime were tortured and murdered en masse. This humanitarian disaster cum genocide, which wiped out a quarter of the population, became known worldwide as "The Killing Fields," the title of a 1984 British film about the Khmer Rouge.

'People who hate technology and want to force the world back to a simple life are a recurring problem,' Armstrong continued. 'If Cambodia was another warning from this mix of socialism and climate, the future doesn't look very bright as we continually have to face these people over and over again.'

Greenpeace uses Greta to promote its own agenda

Greta Thunberg is coached by Jennifer Morgan of Greenpeace, who traveled to the World Economic Forum in Davos with Al Gore (creator of the totally debunked, by all accounts, lie documentary 'An Inconvenient Truth'). 'Greenpeace funds Greta, and their donors consist of a long list of socialists. Greta showed up two days before the election in Alberta, Canada, to tell people that because of climate change they have to give up their jobs.'

'That none of this is getting into the European media at all is even more fascinating. They are not allowed to report on Greta being recruited by Greenpeace, or when she flew to Canada to try to influence the election.'

'Greenpeace has a long history with violence, and now they have Greta to get more attention than ever before. They are strategically very aware that people are more likely to listen to Greta than ever to an adult.'

'Greenpeace is pursuing the same kind of goal that was attempted in Cambodia: back to rural living, an end to fossil fuels (=an end to current prosperity), reducing the population, and an end to technological progress. They are Marxists, just like the Khmer Rouge, but they prefer to call themselves 'progressives,' when in reality they want to impose regression (decline).'

'So, while they launched a huge investigation into how Russia allegedly influenced the U.S. election (for which there was still not a shred of evidence), not one word is devoted to how Greenpeace is using Greta to penetrate governments, and even Davos. Because she is a child, everyone is afraid to criticize her. Jennifer Morgan would NEVER be allowed into Davos on behalf of Greenpeace. Greta is the key to the world. With Greta, they get about $20 million in donations with which they want to impose Greenpeace's agenda on the world.'

'Greenpeace is pursuing the same kind of goal as in Cambodia: a return to rural life, an end to fossil fuels (=an end to current prosperity), population reduction, and an end to technological progress. They are Marxists, just like the Khmer Rouge, but they prefer to call themselves "progressives," when in reality they want to impose regression (backwardness).

'So, while they have launched a huge investigation into how Russia allegedly influenced the U.S. election (for which there was still not a shred of evidence), not a word is said about how Greenpeace is using Greta to invade governments, and even Davos. Because she is a child, everyone is afraid to criticize her. Jennifer Morgan would NEVER be allowed into Davos on behalf of Greenpeace. Greta is the key to the world. With Greta, they get about $20 million in donations with which they want to impose Greenpeace's agenda on the world.

The raw, unaltered data from NASA again clearly shows that there is no climate crisis at all, the annual CO2 change is actually decreasing rather than increasing, and the climate is getting colder. 'Now they are trying to twist everything to claim that they were right after all, and the extreme cold is the result of CO2, when there is no evidence for that. That's not scientific,' Armstrong comments.

'They're just lying about this trend, to push their population control agenda through.' Armstrong was a guest of the White House at a dinner with all the major environmental groups in the 1990s. 'They admitted that their goal is population reduction. CO2 is used to further the same agenda, which is total nonsense... .These people are dishonest, dangerous, and determined to destroy the industrial revolution. They want to send us back to the stone age, and in addition to stopping heating (in NL by cutting off gas) and air conditioning, and brainwashing girls not to have children, they also want to eliminate cars and airplanes.'

It wouldn't be all that bad if this socially and humanly hostile ideology were espoused only by a small left-wing extremist climate sect. However, this sect has managed to penetrate into the highest levels of all Western governments, parliaments and (government) institutions, and has now begun in earnest to break down our prosperity and well-being step by step, with the ultimate goal of eliminating millions of weaklings

and 'dissidents' who refuse to subscribe to or
implement this communist climate agenda.

Chapter 8: Fossil Fuels

'Green New Deal' from rising Democratic star Ocasio-Cortez means 'the eradication of all life on earth' - 'If fossil fuels are banned every tree on earth will be cut down'

Dr. Patrick Moore, co-founder of Greenpeace, has lashed out hard at Alexandria Ocasio-Cortez, the new darling of the 'progressive' left in America. The 'Democratic Socialist' has presented a 'Green New Deal' that will cost tens of billions of dollars and, according to numerous critics, will throw the United States back into a pre-industrial society. Moore tweeted that he finds Ocasio-Cortez a "hypocrite" and a "pompous dork" because implementing her demand to quit fossil fuels-which the European administration has already begun to do with the natural gas shutdown-will cause "mass deaths.

Moore broke with "his" Greenpeace years ago after the environmental movement was taken over from within by far-left anarchists, of which Ocasio-Cortez is an exemplar.

Get rid of all planes and cars

The "Green New Deal," the Green Left's version of Climate Agreement in overdrive, wants the U.S. to completely break with oil, gas and nuclear power. Air travel must be replaced by trains (even across oceans), and 99% of all cars must disappear.

As usual, of course, with the exception of the ruling elite. The New York Post, for example, reports that Ocasio herself has a gigantic "carbon footprint," in part because her campaign team uses regular gasoline cars almost exclusively. She herself took the plane 66 times between May 2017 and December last year, compared to only 18 times by train, to which, if it were up to her, all people would soon be obliged to switch.

Socialist money presses on for free housing

On top of that, every building in the U.S. will have to be thoroughly modified or even rebuilt to meet very stringent climate requirements. Cortez wants to finance millions of government jobs for this purpose. Those who don't want to work, by the way, will be allowed to stay home fully paid and won't have to pay living expenses anymore either. But who would want that?

How does "AOC" plan to pay for its green Utopia? Simple: by simply turning on the money presses, which is the only way to finance its draconian and extremely expensive plans. The fact that this socialism led to widespread poverty and misery all over the world throughout history should not be a name, because "we're going to get it right this time," Cortez said in an earlier interview.

This plan means the eradication of all life.

The Green New Deal even states that all greenhouse gases must be removed from the atmosphere. Moore's response: 'Technically (scientifically) this means removing all water vapor and all CO2, which means the extinction of all life. Brilliant.'

AOC then wrote that 'if you don't like the deal, you should just come up with your own ambitious proposal to solve the global climate crisis. Until then, we're in charge, and you're just shouting from the sidelines.

To which Moore had a firm rebuttal: 'High-falutin' sucker. You don't have any plan to feed 8 billion people without fossil fuels or get the food into the cities. Horses? If fossil fuels are banned then every tree on earth will be cut down for fuel to cook and heat. You will cause mass mortality... You are nothing but a plain old hypocrite, just like the rest, and have ZERO expertise in any area you claim to be able to say anything about.'

In a later response to a tweet from another climate fanatic who claimed that 'the end of fossil fuels is inevitable', Moore wrote: 'You are suffering from delusions if you think fossil fuels will disappear anytime soon. Maybe in 500 years. AOC's attitude is irresponsible and condescending. She is a neophyte

pretending to be smart. Her kind, if put in charge, will
lead us to ruin.'

Chapter 9: Human compost

Time for optimism: Earth is still very empty, there is enough energy and money, and we can use a lot more of CO2.

Released in 1973, the film Soylent Green is considered one of the greater science fiction classics, and won several awards. The film is about the year 2022, in which the earth is plagued by overpopulation, and there are 40 million people living in New York. Ordinary food is scarce and extremely expensive, as is clean water. The common people eat one factory-grown product called Soylent (Soy from soy, Lent from lentils). Of the three varieties, Soylent Green is the best. During a murder investigation, a cop and his roommate make the shocking discovery that Soylent Green is made from human bodies. This horror picture is slowly becoming a reality as the world's first human compost facility opened in the U.S. this year.

"In the sweat of thy face shalt thou eat bread, till thou return unto the ground, because thou wast taken out of it: for dust thou art, and unto dust shall thou return. (Genesis 3:19)

When your time comes, we in the West have two options for our mortal remains: burial or cremation, Science Alert wrote in December 2019. That has now been joined by a "unique alternative ritual": compost.

Recomposting

The first facility to process dead bodies into compost has been built in Seattle. The process is advertised as "recomposting," "natural organic decomposition" and even "life after death.

Founder Katrina Spade called the law, which took effect in May 2020 and made "composting" of human bodies legal, a green "funeral revolution. Recompose's website states that "bodies are covered in wood chips and exposed to the air, creating a perfect environment for natural microbes and beneficial bacteria. In 30 days, the body is completely transformed, creating soil that can be used to grow new life.

Next of kin are encouraged by the company to use some of this human compost in their own gardens. Pomodoro di Nonna: Grandma's tomato soup from her own garden takes on a very literal dimension....

According to Recompose, composting would be more environmentally friendly than burial, and certainly than cremation, because burning a corpse releases CO_2. Opting for compost would save one ton of CO_2, and also eliminate the need to set aside land for cemeteries. Cost of this funeral: $5500.

The transformation of human remains into compost to grow food comes close to the sinister future sketched in the - visually, incidentally, very dated - film Soylent

Green, although of course dead bodies are not yet used directly for food production.

In addition to a chillingly cold form of cannibalism, the almost half-century-old film also shows a ceremonial form of euthanasia, in which people are killed - even forcibly - for the 'good' of society. Just before they receive their injection - euphemistically presented as 'going home' - they are shown a film about the former Earth, how beautiful everything was then.

Especially since 2020, we have seen that with the corona measures, the de-humanization of humans and humanity has accelerated. At best, people are seen as products to be linked to a global digital control system using technology such as 5G and vaccinations. In fact, a significant portion of the international climate movement openly views humans as a burden and a curse, which could be a frightening steppingstone to rationalizing misanthropic government policies, and ultimately justifying and condoning mass genocide, in whatever way it would be carried out.

Time for optimism: Earth is empty, energy and money are plentiful

People have come to take for granted the idea that the earth is "overpopulated" and natural resources are "scarce" thanks to incessant propaganda. However, numerous previous predictions about this have never come true. The infamous Club of Rome in the 1970s predicted a massive global energy, food and resource crisis in the year 2000, but none of it came true.

High time, then, for an optimistic vision of the future. The reality is that the Earth is still very empty. Just look at photos from space - traces of human presence are still barely recognizable, except for a handful of densely populated urban areas. With modern technologies and more CO_2 (whose levels in the atmosphere are still historically, almost dangerously low*), gigantic vast empty areas like Siberia and the Sahara can be transformed into fertile and livable zones, where billions of people can live. Money is plentiful, at least if humanity finally decides to use the annual trillions spent on weaponry and wars for more useful purposes.

There is plenty of energy available, even for tens of billions of people - especially if the rapid development of Thorium and nuclear fusion power plants is fully implemented. Assuming that these become commercially viable around 2050, there will still be more than enough gas, oil, coal, uranium and plutonium for the next 30 years to meet the rapidly growing demand for energy. Even after that, "fossil" sources will be able to provide cheap and reliable energy for a long time to come.

The Modern West is leading us precisely into a scarce and dark future without freedom

The Western-led trend, however, is exactly the opposite; driven by fear and misanthropy bordering on negativity, they want to make energy scarce, unreliable and expensive (solar and wind), just like food and water, which is why the state, the EU, the UN and globalists like Bill Gates are now trying to get their hands on all agricultural land. Those who survive the many crise, which will become inevitable in the coming decades due to these policies, will have to live as slaves without any form of freedom and self-determination, and with only a fraction of today's prosperity, under the yoke of a rock-hard technocratic dictatorship.

The old order is now trying to seize total power through the 'Great Reset' (/ 'Build Back Better'), 'Agenda 2030', the 'Green New Deal' and the Covid-19 vaccination campaigns, and thus realize this dark future. Yet we can still escape it; all it takes is a mass awakening, a mass peaceful resistance, a mass NO. We want another 'Great Reset', one in which the current ruling order is actually removed and loses its power, and ordinary people are finally allowed to really decide for themselves what their own health and their own future, and that of their village, city, country, people, society, economy and culture, should look like.

Our other books

Check out our other books for other unreported news, exposed facts and debunked truths, and more.

Join the exclusive Rebel Press Media Circle!

You will get a new updates about the unreported reality delivered in your inbox every Friday.

Sign up here today:

https://campsite.bio/rebelpressmedia